WHAT MAKES
DAY AND NIGHT

WHAT MAKES DAY AND NIGHT

BY FRANKLYN M. BRANLEY

ILLUSTRATED BY ARTHUR DORROS

HARPER

An Imprint of HarperCollinsPublishers

The Let's-Read-and-Find-Out Science book series was originated by Dr. Franklyn M. Branley, Astronomer Emeritus and former Chairman of the American Museum of Natural History–Hayden Planetarium, and was formerly co-edited by him and Dr. Roma Gans, Professor Emeritus of Childhood Education, Teachers College, Columbia University. Text and illustrations for each of the books in the series are checked for accuracy by an expert in the relevant field. For more information about Let's-Read-and-Find-Out Science books, write to HarperCollins Children's Books, 195 Broadway, New York, NY 10007, or visit our website at www.letsreadandfindout.com.

Let's Read-and-Find-Out Science® is a trademark of HarperCollins Publishers.

WHAT MAKES DAY AND NIGHT

Library of Congress Cataloging-in-Publication Data
Branley, Franklyn Mansfield, date
        What makes day and night.
        (Let's-read-and-find-out science book)
        Summary: A simple explanation of how the rotation of the earth causes night and day.
        ISBN 978-0-06-238197-2
        1. Earth—Rotation—Juvenile literature. 2. Day—Juvenile literature. 2. Night—Juvenile literature.
[1. Earth—Rotation. 2. Day. 3. Night.] I. Dorros, Arthur, ill. II. Title. III. Series.
QB633.B73   1986   85-47903
525'.35

15 16 17 18 19   SCP   10 9 8 7 6 5 4 3 2 1
❖
Revised edition, 2015

We all live on the earth.

The earth is our planet.
It is round like a big ball.
And it is spinning.

It's hard to believe the earth is always turning, because we don't feel any motion. This is because the earth spins smoothly—always at the same speed.

This is a photograph of the earth. It was taken by a camera aboard the Apollo 17 spacecraft. You can see that the earth is round.

If you were way out in space and watching the earth, you would see it spin. The earth spins around once in twenty-four hours.

Light from the sun falls on one-half of the spinning earth. The half in the light has day. The other half is dark. It is in the earth's shadow. That half has night.

As the earth spins we move through the light, into the darkness, and back again. We have day and night.

Imagine you are in a spaceship high above the North Pole. Imagine you can stay there twenty-four hours and watch the earth make one complete turn.

North Pole

South Pole

As the earth turns we have sunrise, daylight, sunset, and night.

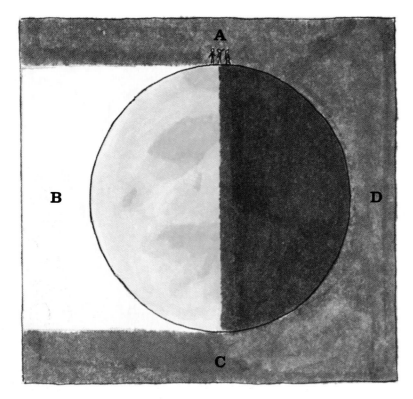

People at A have sunrise.

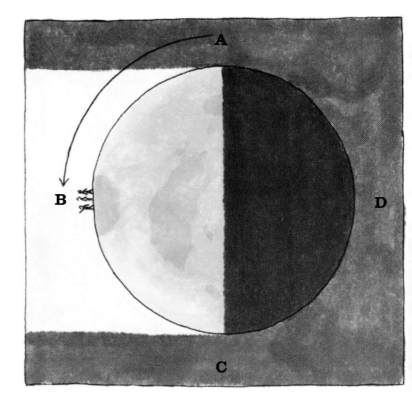

Later, because the earth is turning, they are at B. It is the middle of the day for them. It is noontime.

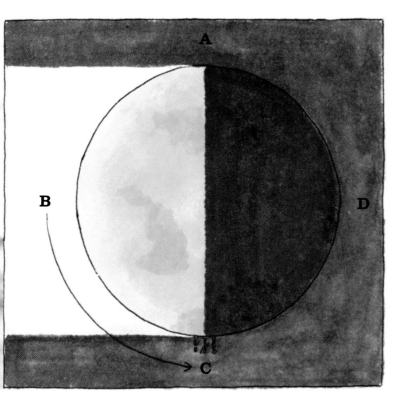

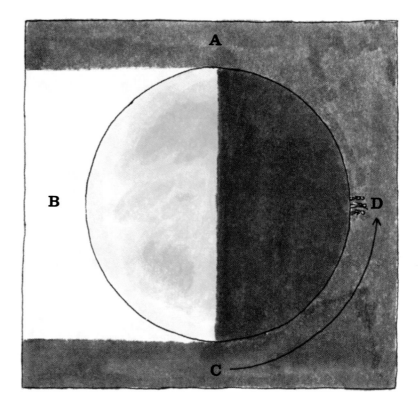

As the earth turns, it carries them to C. They have sunset.

By the time they reach D it is the middle of the night for them. It is midnight. At the end of twenty-four hours they have sunrise again.

You can see how we move from daylight to darkness
by doing an experiment. You will be the earth, and a
lamp will be the sun.

sunrise

day

Stand so that your left side is toward the lamp. Hold your arms out all the way. Your left hand points toward the lamp.

This is sunrise.

Stay in the same spot. Keep your arms out from your sides, and turn to your left. Now the lamp is in front of you. It is the middle of the day. It is noontime.

sunset

night

Keep turning until your right hand points toward the lamp. You are turning away from the light. It is sunset.

Keep turning until your back is toward the lamp. It is night. But your back is in daylight. Half of you is always light, and half is dark. It's the same with the earth.

23

The earth is always turning. It never stops. Round and round it goes. And it goes very fast. About 1000 miles an hour. As the earth turns we are always moving from day to night. And from night to day.

You can see this happen. If you are awake very early, you can see sunrise. The earth is moving you toward the sun.

The earth keeps turning. Later in the day we begin to turn away from the sun. You can see sunset.

About twenty-four hours after sunrise, the sun will rise again. It all happens because the earth is spinning around.

As the earth turns, the sun seems to move across the sky.

If you were on the moon, you would also have day and night. But the moon spins very slowly, so days and nights are long. Places on the moon have two weeks of daylight and then two weeks of darkness.

During one night on the moon the earth spins around fourteen times.

The turning earth gives us about twelve hours of daylight and twelve hours of darkness. That seems just about right for all of us on the planet earth.

FIND OUT MORE ABOUT WHAT MAKES DAY AND NIGHT

- Locate your city on a globe. Pick a time of day for your city and compare that time of day with the time in another place. What different things are people doing around the world when you are eating lunch? Sleeping?

- A calendar is based on the movements of the earth, the sun, and the moon. Even though we all live on the same earth, not all countries around the world have the same calendars. What other calendars do other cultures use? How do they compare to our calendar? How are the lengths of a day, a month, and a year related to the sun-earth-moon system?

- What animals and bugs do you see in the daylight, and which do you see at night? Before you leave home in the morning, walk outside and write down which animals or bugs you see. Walk the same route at night. What do you see? Hear? Why do you think some animals come out in the day and some at night?

- Choose a spot to observe the sun every morning, noontime, and late afternoon. Create a chart that shows the position of the sun relative to the surrounding landscape at each of these times. How does the sun move? Which direction does it move in? Compare your findings from month to month.

- Visit http://www.nasa.gov for more information on space, the earth, and our sun.